# Emergency Vehicles
# Police Cars

## Chris Oxlade

QEB Publishing

Published in the United States by
QEB Publishing, Inc.
3 Wrigley, Suite A
Irvine, CA 92618

www.qeb-publishing.com

Library of Congress Cataloging-in-Publication Data

Oxlade, Chris.
  Police car / Chris Oxlade.
      p. cm. -- (QEB emergency vehicles)
  Includes index.
  ISBN 978-1-59566-976-6 (hardcover)
  1. Police vehicles--Juvenile literature. I. Title.
  HV7936.V4.O95 2010
  363.2'32--dc22
                                          2009005879

ISBN 978-1-59566-246-0 (paperback)

Printed and bound in the United States of America in North Mankato, Minnesota

092809

QED 10-2009 7

**Author** Chris Oxlade
**Project Editor** Eve Marleau
**Designer** Susi Martin

**Publisher** Steve Evans
**Creative Director** Zeta Davies
**Managing Editor** Amanda Askew

**Picture credits**
(t=top, b=bottom, l=left, r=right, c=center, fc=front cover)

**Alamy**
4l Goss images; 6–7 Paul Springett A; 7r Justin Kase zfourz; 8–9 Howard Sayer; 10 ACE STOCK LIMITED; 11 Jack Sullivan; 12–13 fine art
**Chris Taylor, with thanks to the Metropolitan Police**
16–17, 17l
**Corbis**
9r DiMaggio/Kalish
**Photolibrary**
13r Thomas Frey
**Shutterstock**
1; 4–5 MalibuBooks; 14–15 Samuel Acosta; 15 Andresr; 18–19 Denise Kappa; 19r michael rubin; 21r Nicholas Rjabow; 20l Jenny Woodworth
**www.ukemergency.co.uk**
20–21

Words in **bold** can be found in the glossary on page 23.

# Contents

# What is a police car?

A police car is an **emergency** vehicle driven by police officers. They use police cars to control **traffic**, **patrol** the streets, and chase criminals.

Not all police cars are big and fast. This is an electric city patrol car.

Police cars are different from normal cars. They often have bigger engines, and better brakes and tires.

# Lights and sirens

Police cars have flashing lights and noisy **sirens**. Red and blue flashing lights warn other drivers that a police car is coming. Loud sirens make long screeching noises or beeps.

Police cars have colorful blocks and stripes, so they can easily be seen.

Some of the markings on police cars are **reflective**, which makes them shine at night. The markings make the cars easy for people to recognize.

A police officer uses lights and sirens to make sure people can see and hear the car.

# Police car
# equipment

Police cars have a lot of special equipment inside, including a **two-way radio**. Police officers use the radio to talk to other officers or the police headquarters.

These police officers in the UK are using their two-way radio to report an **incident**.

Some police cars have a small **computer terminal** inside. It gives police officers information about **suspects** and their cars.

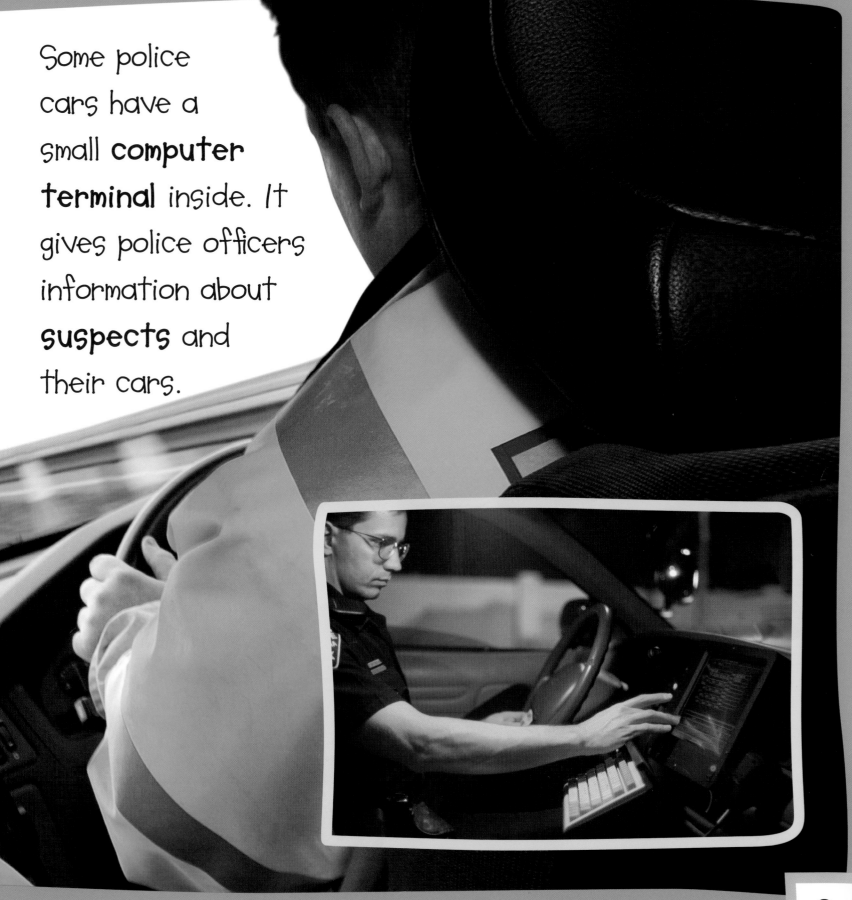

# High-speed cars

A pursuit car is a very fast police car. Police officers use them to chase criminals. Pursuit cars are usually powerful sports cars.

This Italian pursuit car is a Maserati sports car.

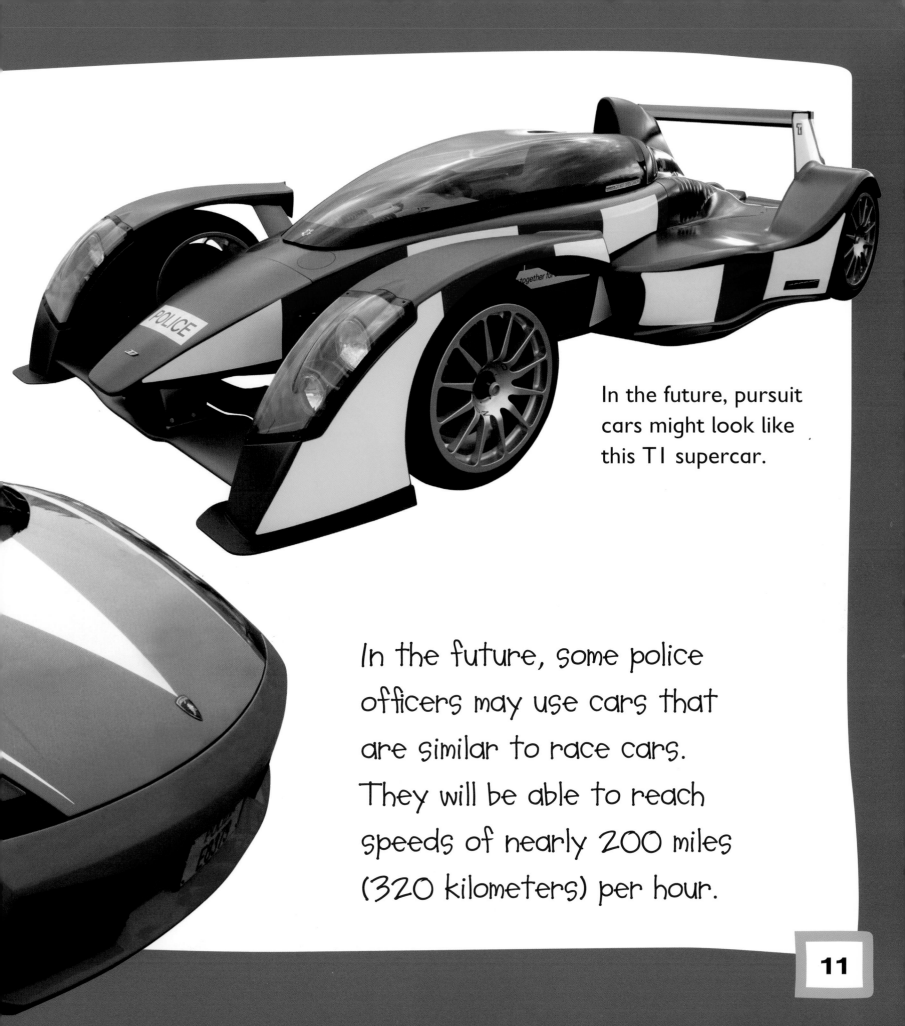

In the future, pursuit cars might look like this T1 supercar.

In the future, some police officers may use cars that are similar to race cars. They will be able to reach speeds of nearly 200 miles (320 kilometers) per hour.

# Special police cars

Police forces also have special-purpose cars. Some forces have rescue cars with **four-wheel drive** for going **off road**. They can be used to reach people on ground, such as sand, that normal cars cannot easily drive on.

Other special police vehicles include mobile police command centers or armored trucks for controlling large crowds.

This four-wheel drive police car is used on the beaches in California.

# Police vans

Police forces have vans for transporting people and equipment. Some police forces have teams of officers who deal with dangerous criminals who carry weapons. They travel in armored vans.

This police van has a
windshield protector.

Some vans are
used for taking
police officers and
suspects to where
they are needed.

An armored van is
built in a special way,
so it is protected
against attack.

# Driving a police car

Police officers have to drive fast when they are chasing suspects. This can be dangerous for the police officers and other drivers on the road, so they are specially trained to drive at high speeds.

Police officers must be able to control a car in any type of weather.

Police officers go to special driving schools. They learn the skills they need to drive safely at high speed, to stop quickly, and to control the car if they skid.

Police officers practice driving with two wheels off the road.

# Police on two wheels

Police officers use motorcycles as well as cars. Motorcycles are good for moving through traffic on busy city streets. Traffic officers use them for patrolling highways and for riding alongside cars transporting important people.

A highway patrol motorcycle.

Town and city police officers can travel more quickly by bicycle than on foot.

# Land, air, and sea

The police also use aircraft, horses, and boats. Police use helicopters to follow criminals on the ground and to check for traffic jams. Police officers ride horses to patrol the streets.

Police officers are often seen on horseback in towns and cities.

Police use motorboats to patrol rivers and shorelines in cities. They can search suspicious boats and rescue people from the water.

# Activities

- Which picture shows a pursuit car, a police boat, and a police motorcycle?

- Make a drawing of your favorite police car. What kind of car is it? Does it have lights and sirens? What color is it?

- Write a story about a police chase. It could be anywhere in the world— or even on another planet! What car would you drive? What crime would you be fighting? How dangerous would it be? How long would it take?

- Which of these police cars would be used to control a large crowd?

# Glossary

**Computer terminal**
A machine that lets people look at information stored on a computer.

**Emergency**
A dangerous situation that must be dealt with right away.

**Four-wheel drive**
Where all the wheels of a vehicle are turned by the engine.

**Incident**
Something that happens.

**Off road**
When a vehicle can be used on rough ground.

**Patrol**
To walk or drive around an area several times to check for trouble or danger.

**Reflective**
A material that light bounces off very well.

**Siren**
A machine that makes a loud, screeching noise.

**Suspect**
Someone who the police think is guilty of committing a crime.

**Traffic**
Cars, trucks, motorcycles, and other vehicles on the road.

**Two-way radio**
A radio set that lets people talk to each other.

# Index